# Insight for Adult Learning Groups

Module 23

*General Editor: David G. Hamilton*

# Can we trust the Bible?

David G. Hamilton

**Insight for Adult Learning Groups**

Module 23

*General Editor: David G. Hamilton*

Marshall Pickering
*An Imprint of* HarperCollins*Publishers*

Marshall Pickering is an Imprint of
HarperCollins *Religious*
Part of HarperCollins *Publishers*
77–85 Fulham Palace Road, London W6 8JB

First published in Great Britain
in 1996 by Marshall Pickering

1 3 5 7 9 10 8 6 4 2

Copyright © 1996 David G. Hamilton

David G. Hamilton asserts the moral right to be
identified as the author of this work

A catalogue record for this book is
available from the British Library

0 551 030399

Printed and bound in Great Britain by
Woolnough Bookbinding Limited, Irthlingborough, Northamptonshire

# Contents

Preface vi

Introduction vii


*Session 1*  Putting the Bible in its place 1

*Session 2*  The Bible at a glance 7

*Session 3*  The Bible in the Church 13

*Session 4*  The God of the Bible 19

# Preface

*INSIGHT* is a learning programme for the *whole* Church. It incorporates learning resources for use with children, teenagers, younger adults, adult learning groups, intergenerational groups and church holiday clubs for young people. Its locus is the community of faith, people of all ages engaged in worshipping, learning and serving God together. The programme offers a wide range of learning modules for each of the constituent groups and encourages congregational leaders to identify the needs of their people and to construct their own parish education programme on a *pick 'n' mix* basis using the modules. The scheme is outlined in the *INSIGHT Handbook* and *INSIGHT for Church Leaders*.

The modules in this series of volumes, *INSIGHT for Adult Learning Groups*, offer a wide range of studies which range in content from the personal and pastoral needs of individuals to the major social issues of the day and the challenge to Christians to engage in creative and redemptive discipleship. Some adult learning groups may be attracted also to the options available in the series of titles in the companion series, *INSIGHT for Younger Adults*.

The series has been developed by Parish Education Publications in partnership with HarperCollins*Religious*.

DAVID G. HAMILTON
GENERAL EDITOR

# Introduction

This module touches upon a vast and important subject for Christians and non-Christians alike; namely, how we regard the Bible today. The four study sessions are intended to provide enough introductory comment to stimulate further study and discussion in small groups. The module is divided into four study sessions for convenience but it may be desirable to extend the programme to six meetings or more.

Since all members of the group should have copies of this study guide it may be appropriate to share the leadership of the sessions on a rotation basis. It would be helpful if the session leader engaged in some further 'in depth' study by way of preparation; to this end some helpful titles are listed below. Clearly, for this module, the principle resource is the Bible itself. It would be useful to have alternative English translations to hand. At the start of this programme, it would be interesting to display copies of a Hebrew Bible and a Greek New Testament. A good bible atlas would also assist in locating places of significance. Other books of possible interest are grouped according to areas of interest.

### Bible background

*The Lion Encyclopaedia of the Bible*, Pat Alexander (ed.), Lion, 1978.
*The Natural History of the Land of the Bible*, Alan Azaria, Doubleday, 1978.
*Ancient Israel: Its Life and Institutions*, Roland De Vaux, Darton, Longman & Todd, 1988.
*Collins Bible Handbook*, Jacques Musset, Collins Liturgical Publications, 1988.
*The New Manners and Customs of Bible Times*, Ralph Gower, Moody Press, 1987.
*The Student's Atlas of the Bible*, Paternoster, undated.

**Interpreting the Bible**

*Escaping from Fundamentalism*, James Barr, SCM, 1984.

*The Bible without Illusions*, R. P. C. & A. T. Hanson, SCM/Trinity, 1989.

*The Use and Abuse of the Bible*, Dennis Nineham, Macmillan, 1976.

*A Basic Introduction to the Old Testament* and *A Basic Introduction to the New Testament*, Robert C. Walton, SCM, 1980.

# Putting the Bible in its place

AIM

To consider the essential nature of the Bible, to introduce the notion of reliability and to express the expectations of the Bible held by contemporary readers.

STARTER

### What is it we are asked to trust?

The Bible as we know it today is a book: a single volume of miscellaneous writings spanning over one thousand years of religious history that gave rise both to Judaism and Christianity. The Bible is a collection of writings edited into a work in two parts – the Old Testament and the New Testament. The dominant theme is the human experience of God. Although it contains many sub-themes, the Bible can be viewed overall as a record of how the ancients in a particular society perceived and related to God.

However, over the long period of its development and throughout the Christian era, the Bible has been regarded as something rather more than a document of historical value and interest. Christians have regarded the Bible as an authoritative source for contemporary living. Phrases commonly used in the Christian tradition which refer directly to the Bible include 'the living Word', the 'Word of God', 'Holy Scripture' and – for an older generation – simply, 'the Book'. (The Greek word *biblos* is commonly translated as 'book'.) In courts of law, witnesses will swear an oath to tell the truth by placing their hand upon a copy of the Bible – an indication of the reverence in which the Bible is held, even today.

The Bible has a special place in Western society and has undoubtedly been a major influence in the shaping and usage of European languages, art, architecture, music and, indeed, all the expressive arts. The Bible was indivisible from the rise of European culture that came to be labelled Christendom. The practice and development of the Christian religion was heavily dependent upon a more or less common understanding of the Bible, and European civilisation was derived in large measure from its accommodation of the Christian religion. In today's secular world, which has seen the end of Christendom and the breakdown of Christianity as a dominant influence, the Bible still commands respect both as a symbol and as an inspiration for living a Christian lifestyle in a pluralist society. Our task here is to ask in what respects we may claim that the Bible has relevance for our contemporary world. What sort of authority does it have? How, in the light of modern understanding, are we to regard the Bible? What is it we are asked to trust?

## FOR REFLECTION AND DISCUSSION

On your own (3 minutes)

Think about what the Bible means to you. Jot down the main points that occur to you.

In small groups (15 minutes)

- Share your initial thoughts and build a composite picture of how your group regards the Bible. It will help if you create a checklist on a flipchart.
- Consider what snags or problems you see in trusting the Bible as a guide for living today. Again, create a checklist. You may wish to preserve this chart for future reference.
- To what extent would you, as a group, trust the Bible?

### What does it mean to trust a book?

If we trust an atlas or a book of road maps we do so believing that they offer us *accurate* geographical information. We are prepared to rely upon a map when planning a journey. If we refer to a bus timetable, we are prepared to believe that the contents are entirely reliable and not simply the guesswork or speculation of some detached author. In each of these examples, the volume is consulted precisely because it is deemed to be reliable. Its provenance is assured by the authority which issued it. Such books either are factual or they state guaranteed intentions. They include dictionaries and encyclopaedias, for example. They are trustworthy in the sense that we may, with complete confidence, plan and base future actions upon the information provided. That kind of book is rather different from a novel or a book of poetry where the authors appeal to our own experience of life and invite us to exercise our imagination by entering into a world of ideas and experiences which is sometimes hypothetical, sometimes plausible and, on other occasions, utterly fantastic. This is the world of literature.

In between factual books and fiction or poetry books, there is a vast category of non-fiction, which focuses on the enquiry into the phenomenon of life in all its aspects. Think of the science of virology: how much do scientists know and how much have they yet to discover about viruses? It is a field of knowledge still in development; we trust medical practitioners who tell us that we 'have a virus', recognising implicitly that their diagnosis is based upon 'state of the art' awareness. Not so long ago, keyhole and laser surgery were unthinkable. Present indications suggest that brain surgery will, in the future, be regarded as a barbaric practice. Thirty years from now, the textbooks currently being studied by medical students will be historical curiosities. To sum up: in science, as in other spheres of knowledge, we anticipate development. Optimistically, we call it 'progress'. Those who attempt to make sense of our world and of the human condition write books to share their ideas and to advance our corporate understanding.

The extent to which we trust – that is, rely upon – a particular work will vary according to the discipline: an astronomer's actual description of our galaxy is one thing, but a speculative suggestion as to how our galaxy – or, indeed, the universe – came into being is quite another. Each has its own level of trustworthiness which becomes a matter for careful reflection and assessment.

The Bible is no different in this essential respect. It is a collection of writings, written in varying circumstances and at different times in the course of the millennium before, and incorporating, the time of Christ. Many of these writings have some degree of historical basis; some are works of fiction; some are epic poems; and others are poems intended to be sung. All these writings have something in common: they need to be interpreted in the light of the situations and circumstances that caused them to be written in the first place.

By asking what prompted particular authors to put stylus to scroll, we are able to discern what meaning the writings would hold to the authors' peers. By asking in what respects the essential meaning of these passages continues to be of significance and value to later generations, not least our own, we are in a position to reach a sober estimate of the value of these writings for us.

The key to such an evaluation of the Christian scriptures is in how we interpret them. If we treat everything in the Bible as undisputed fact we shall soon run into trouble. Equally, if we dismiss out of hand the claim that there is, indeed, much factual and historically accurate information in the Bible, we are unlikely to find very much of value in its pages – other than an appreciation of some of its purple passages in English translation as being of literary merit.

The reality is that the Bible is a collection of writings of antiquity which need to be read in the context from which they originate; they also may be read for meanings which in essence are timeless and which transcend cultural and historical boundaries. It is by subjecting the contents of the Bible to careful and intelligent reading that it becomes trustworthy, inspiring and enabling.

In small groups (10 minutes)

Read Psalm 145.

- What does it tell us about the author's experience of God? To what extent is this a factual, scientific statement? In what ways is it the entirely subjective view of one individual?
- What do you think of the psalmist's use of imagery?
- What 'big' meaning or overview do you take from the psalm as something that is as true for you today as it was for this ancient writer?
- How do we in the Church use this psalm in devotions and worship?

**A question of reliability**

The Protestant Bible, as we know it today, is divided into two parts: the Old Testament and the New Testament; the version used by the Roman Catholic Church and other denominations also includes a number of writings known collectively as the Apocrypha. The writings of the Old Testament were originally composed in Hebrew or – in some instances – Aramaic, but before the time of Jesus they had been translated (not always accurately) into Greek. This Greek version, known as the Septuagint, was used most frequently as a source for those first Christians whose writings in Greek were eventually to form what we now call the New Testament. These writings were translated into Latin at an early stage, and the subsequent development of the Bible as an agreed and definitive set of writings, recognised by the Church as Scripture, depended for many centuries upon them.

When analysing the origins of the Christian Bible, it is important to recognise a number of basic facts:

- Even the earliest versions of these writings were available to most people in translation.
- All copies of the writings were scripted by hand and so the possibility (and reality) of human error was considerable. There is a whole field of scholarship given over to the comparison of ancient texts where variant readings vie for authenticity.
- The process of development of these writings was, from the beginning, subject to modification and a change of emphasis by a succession of editors.
- Those who wrote the original works and edited later versions did so with a particular agenda in mind; for example, whether to write in favour of a Hebrew monarchy or to write against it, preferring a loose federation of autonomous tribes.
- Whatever we think about the authors being inspired by God to write as they did, the fact remains that the writings of the Bible are the product of human endeavour and reflect the opinions, insights, convictions, feelings, experience and faith of the individuals who wrote them.

Yet, for all this, the Christian Church is happy to claim that in the Bible we find inspiration for the contemporary religious life. Clearly, for most Christians, the Bible is held to be reliable. But how reliable? How should it be read? How far can we go along with its stories and claims and prescriptions for living a godly life?

In groups (20 minutes)

- Using three or four different English translations of the Bible (the *Authorised Version*, *Good News Bible*, *New English Bible* and the *New International Bible*) compare a number of well-known passages (for example, Genesis 1, Exodus 3, Psalm 23, Mark 16:14–20 and Philippians 2:1–11). How important are the differences in translation? Are there differences in meaning or simply differences in style?

- What do you consider to be the hallmarks of a good English translation? Make a list on the flipchart and retain this for future reference.
- When you read the Bible what do you look for? Why do you read it? Is it simply a matter of using the Bible as a ready reckoner? In what way do you trust the Bible?

# The Bible at a glance

To introduce the need for careful study of the Bible, with particular regard to the structure and background of the writings inherited by the modern Church.

**Some tools for the bible detective**

No book in the entire history of world literature has been subjected to the same intensive scrutiny as the Christian Bible. Those who regard the Bible as Holy Scripture have examined it, sentence by sentence, in an effort to understand it in its original context and to interpret its meaning for today. Modern versions of the Bible contain a ready reckoner reference system. The books of the Bible, unless very brief, are divided into verses. The standard system of annotation – for example,'John 3:16' – allows the reader to find a particular passage with relative ease. Originally, however, there was no such system of reference. Indeed, some writings – now split into *two* books such as 1 and 2 Samuel and 1 and 2 Kings – were once single composite works.

This knowledge serves to remind us that in reading the Bible we do well to retain an overview and to view each book as a whole. For the modern churchgoer this is not as self-evident or as trite as it may appear. After all, the common practice in public worship is to read several brief portions from different parts of the Bible. These 'lections' are often deemed to be appropriate to the theme of the service. (A glance at a modern lectionary for use in public worship will readily stimulate debate as to the relevance of some prescribed readings for the exploration of a particular theme!) This 'bits and pieces' approach to bible reading may have its place where it is assumed that worshippers have an extensive knowledge of the Bible and so will readily place each reading in context. In our day and generation, however, no such assumptions are warranted.

Seeing the Bible as a 'whole' is important. For example, some group members will find it an interesting experience to read an entire Gospel at one sitting. By doing so, certain trends become clear and we grasp something of the author's intention and style. Read the Gospel of John and discover the writer's constant rebuke to 'the Jews', that is, those who did not convert to Christianity. The writer was, of course, not being anti-Semitic as such, yet later generations in the Christian Church quoted many of the sayings in this Gospel as justification for persecution of Jewish communities. Look at the style of the author of this Gospel, in particular at the structure of the 'I am' sayings following on as punchlines at the end of particular stories. Notice that although John's Gospel does not contain a direct account of the Last Supper on the eve of Passover, the whole of the book is shot through with a scarcely veiled eucharistic motif. Seeing each book of the Bible as a whole is an important way of grasping the overriding point being made by the author.

## FOR REFLECTION AND DISCUSSION

In groups (15 minutes)

Read the following stories (if time is short you may wish to allocate particular passages to individuals or pairs):

> John 6:1–15; 25–35
> John 10:1–9
> John 10:11–16
> John 14:1–7

List the theme of each story and the 'punchline' associated with it. Compare the style and structure in each case and identify what is common to the approach.

**Too many cooks?**

We have a saying that 'too many cooks spoil the broth'. Groups may wish to decide whether it applies to the Bible. For those who seek slick, factual, incontrovertible answers to life's questions, the saying may ring true. For those who are prepared to adopt a more reflective approach, the real complexity of the Bible will prove fascinating.

The fact is that many books in the Bible, particularly in the Old Testament, are the work of not one but a number of authors. For example, the Psalms (once known as 'the Psalms of David') are a collection of songs written by many different people over several centuries. While it seems clear that King David did write some songs and probably played an influential part in collecting a number of the court or royal psalms, he certainly did not compose them all. Virtually all reputable bible scholars recognise that the 'book' of the prophet Isaiah falls into at least three parts, each written by a different author and in different circumstances. It is very important, in order to appreciate the work fully, to know that chapters 1–39 were written in Jerusalem prior to the exile of the leaders of Judah (the southern kingdom) to Babylon, whereas later chapters refer to the captivity in Babylon and to the eventual resettlement in Jerusalem. The later authors stood in the same prophetic line as the first Isaiah.

The first five books of the Old Testament (known as the 'Pentateuch') are – in Jewish tradition – the books of the Law. Again, these are the work of a number of writers, sometimes writing around the same time but in different places and from very distinctive points of view. In the Bible as we now have it, however, these different strands have been woven into a unified tapestry. Even so, there is evidence of repetition and of alternate, sometimes inconsistent, accounts of the same event being allowed to stand side by side.

In groups (15 minutes)

Compare the following passages:

Exodus 20:1–17 and Deuteronomy 5:1–22
Exodus 14:13–31 and Joshua 3 and 2 Kings 2:5–15
1 Samuel 31 and 1 Chronicles 10
1 Samuel 8 and 1 Samuel 9:15–16

The same trend continues throughout the Bible. In Judges, the tactic of gaining possession of the promised land of Canaan seems to be one of infiltration and guerrilla warfare, whereas in Joshua much more emphasis is placed upon occupation following major military campaigns and invasions. From earliest Sunday School days every churchgoer knows that David killed Goliath. But compare 1 Samuel 17:41–51 with 2 Samuel 21:19: two similar but different traditions exist side by side.

Alternate accounts are not confined to the Old Testament; in the four Gospels many stories are subject to variation. In the first three Gospels we are told that, towards the end of his ministry, Jesus enters the Temple in Jerusalem and drives out the corrupt money changers and dealers in sacrificial livestock. Yet, in the Gospel of John, Jesus is portrayed as doing this at the outset of his public ministry several years earlier. Which account, if any, is historically correct? Such an example reminds us that the authors of the various writings in the Bible had their own theological, liturgical and literary agenda in mind when they wrote. We should also remember that they did not set out to contribute an essay to a volume commissioned by a publisher! It was not their concern to check the detail of one account against another. The works of these writers were brought together precisely because of their proven worth in rehearsing in some way part of the story of God's people.

### Hebrew origins

Some scholars are uncomfortable when Christians talk about 'the Bible' when they actually are referring to the Old and New Testaments taken together. They point out that, strictly speaking, the Bible comprises the scriptures of the Jewish faith. They will not even permit the term 'Old Testament' but prefer to speak of the 'former' testament. The point is valid in so far as the 'former' testament is a primary resource for the three great religions of Judaism, Christianity and Islam. On this understanding the book at the heart of the Christian religion is referred to as the Christian Bible.

Certainly, in an age of pluralism and political correctness such a designation overcomes the difficulty of claiming that the Bible of the Jews is incomplete; yet, there are many Christians who would say that any religion which does not recognise the Christian scriptures is inadequate and that only in Jesus Christ may we see the completion and fulfilment of God's purpose. Those holding to this exclusive view will find support in the New Testament in various sayings attributed to Jesus; for example, John 14:6b: Jesus is claimed as the only way to God the Father.

In the Jewish tradition, the Hebrew Bible is divided into three parts – Law, Prophets and Writings. In the Gospels of the New Testament, there is ample evidence of Jesus quoting from all three areas of the scriptures. It seems clear that in composing their Gospels, the evangelists used the Hebrew scriptures in a self-fulfilling way. This is not to deny the authentic strand of promise and fulfilment which runs through the Old and New Testaments taken together, but simply to demonstrate that the Gospel writers, in proclaiming the importance of Jesus, were anxious to place him in the context of his Jewish origins and in the monotheistic tradition of Judaism. Indeed, as a number of scholars have pointed out, had Jesus of Nazareth never lived, it would still be possible – based upon a proof-texting approach to the Old Testament – to construct a storyline essentially along the lines of the story of Jesus.

In groups (20 minutes)

- When we read John 14:6b – that no one comes to the Father except through Jesus – how do we relate this to the need to have respect for holy writings and traditions of other world religions?
- How much of the story of Jesus do you think can be 'constructed' from the law, prophecies and writings of the Old Testament?
- In your view, are the promises of God in the Old Testament fulfilled in the New Testament? How do you understand this relationship?

**The person of Jesus**

The reality is that Jesus did live as a real, historical person; of that there is no doubt. This does not mean that we have a detailed historical or biographical account of his life; quite the reverse. In this respect, it is important to recognise the distinctive nature of those writings we know as Gospels. They are not factual biographies; they are not even hagiographies. We have no idea what Jesus looked like and very little knowledge of his origins beyond a few snippets relating to his birth and childhood (which are clearly later additions and motivated by theological considerations to authenticate the divinity of Jesus).

The true nature of a Gospel is to say why Jesus is important for us. The word 'gospel' means 'good news'. The Gospels proclaim the unique significance of Jesus as God incarnate. They dwell on the significant teachings of Jesus over a relatively short period of several years of public activity, and focus mainly on the final days of his life and upon his death. They conclude with the adamant and triumphal claim that God raised Jesus to new life in which his followers may also share.

Perhaps in the Gospels more than anywhere else in the Bible, sympathetic readers face difficult questions of interpretation. For example, what may be taken as historical? What may be regarded as symbolic or theological? What is a sincere attempt, after the fact, to support the early Church concerning Jesus? Here, particularly, it is important to enquire about the context and purpose of the four Gospels. Each has a point of view; for all their superficial sameness they are markedly different from each other.

Such considerations simply highlight the reality that the interpretation of the Gospels is not as straightforward or as clear-cut as some might think. There is room for constructive debate. There are few easy answers. Yet, for all that, across the four Gospels there is remarkable consistency in testifying to the basic elements of the early Church's received tradition: that God reveals himself in Jesus and that faith in God is enhanced and enriched through personal and collective allegiance to Jesus as Christ and Lord.

In groups (15 minutes)

- Do you find it regrettable that we have little 'hard evidence' about the details of the life of Jesus?
- In the light of the argument put forward above, do you think Christians should agree to differ on questions of interpretation of the Bible or would that be to compromise our beliefs and commitment?

# The Bible in the Church

To examine the essential relationship between the origins of the Church and of the Christian Bible and to explore the Church's use of the Bible both in worship and as a record of faith in God.

### The Church's Book

Just as we may say that the Bible gave rise to the Church, so we may also claim that the Church gave rise to the Bible. This statement deserves explanation. The Christian Church is first and foremost a community of faith, for which the Greek word *koinonia*, often given in English as 'fellowship', has no adequate translation. It is a people bound together by God's grace and love who, with a faith and a purpose in common, have developed a corporate identity as the people of God. The word *ekklesia*, meaning an assembly or gathering of people who are called by God to worship and serve him, gives another perspective. It stems from the Greek verb *kalein*, 'to call'.

Therefore, in being the Church, there is a sense of being called by God to be his people and this bears a sense of being distinctive, special and 'set apart'. There is also a strong sense of community, of belonging to one another and to God. Thirdly, the Church is distinctively focused on Jesus Christ who is declared to be its head. Paul likens the Church to a body of many parts with Christ as the head.

The identification of the Jesus of history with the Christ of God, the interpretation by the first followers of Jesus of his crucifixion as *victory* over death, and of his continuing influence – whether interpreted as exaltation or bodily resurrection by the power of God – make Jesus the 'cornerstone' of the new phenomenon, the new age in which God's purposes are being fulfilled.

Whatever way we look at it, the *new* people of God – the *reconstructed* people of God, the new *Israel* – is the *Christian* Church. Not only does the faith of responsive, individual believers prove to be effective for their development as persons, but their corporate faith proves capable of generating the most creative expansion of benevolent activity. This can be identified as mutual caring and responsibility, a sense of social justice, a generosity of spirit and a process of self-emptying and commitment to others – individually and collectively – that we know as the deepest and most sublime expression of love (*agape*). This is the movement that generated many writings reflecting on the good news of Jesus in its many aspects. Many such writings were gospels but only four of these gained the status of 'holy scripture'. Similarly, of the various histories and pseudo-histories, only one such work, 'the Acts of the Apostles', found its way into the accepted collection as scripture. Similarly, of all the many letters or epistles written in the opening decades of the infant Church, only a handful found their way into the Christian Bible. Some of these documents were lost; others were judged to be flawed, inferior, heretical or simply saying nothing new. Scholars refer to this selection process as the 'canon' (meaning 'rule') of scripture – the acid test, as it were, of what was considered worthy and what was usually considered as having been inspired by God. In fact, canonisation of the new scriptures was a slow process lasting several centuries.

The point, however, is that it was the Church – through its leaders and after much prayer, study and debate – that defined what would constitute the generally accepted body of writings we know as the New Testament. At the same time, the Church endorsed the judgement of the apostles that the Hebrew scriptures remained of central significance for the new people of God. It took a considerable time before the relationship between the Old and New Testaments was established, but when it was defined it was in terms of promise and fulfilment. In defining its authoritative sources the Church was also defining itself, and in that sense the Book created the Church.

## FOR REFLECTION AND DISCUSSION

In groups (20 minutes)

- To what extent would you say that the Church, in creating the Gospels, read back into the life and teaching of Jesus ideas that originate not so much with Jesus but with his followers? Consider this question above in the light of Matthew 16:13–20 compared with Mark 8:27–30.
- Look at the words of the Apostle's Creed (see, for example, hymn 546 in *The Church Hymnary, Third Edition*), and say which elements are unambiguously founded on the Bible.

### Using the Bible in worship

Worship is an essentially corporate activity focused on God as Creator, Sustainer, Deliverer and Lord. It is an act of communion or fellowship with God so that we can sing such hymns as 'We are one in the Spirit'. Worship is capable of employing all the expressive arts but if it is to convey meaning it is dependent to a large extent on language and the expression of ideas. It is hardly surprising, therefore, that the words and ideas of the Bible supply the essential vocabulary of worship. Likewise, it is hardly surprising that whole passages of scripture are paraphrased as prayers or set to music as hymns. Both for the old faith community and for the new faith community, songs of praise, faith and renewal were of central importance for the edification or upbuilding of the people through worship; it is not in the least surprising to find such songs included both in the Old Testament and in the New Testament.

The development of worship in the Church centred on the Word of God. Portions of scripture were read or recited as a means of bringing to mind one or other aspect of the saving activity of God in Christ. Just as in the Jewish tradition, readings were taken from the Law (or *Torah*), the Prophets and the Writings, so in the Christian Church there emerged the practice of reading from the Old Testament, the epistles (or letters) and, supremely, the Gospels. Also in this way, the Church strove – not always successfully – to present a consistent thematic approach using the three selected lections. Following the Reformation, the prominence of the scriptures became more pronounced. In the Scottish Presbyterian tradition this is exemplified in the development of the Metrical Psalms and the singing of the Word of God – the rehearsing of the tradition in song.

In groups (20 minutes)

Consider the following passages as liturgical 'set pieces'. Discuss how they might have been used in worship. How do we use them today?

- Genesis 1:1–2:4a (the Creation Hymn)
- Colossians 1:15–20 (part of a baptismal liturgy)
- Matthew 6:9–13 (the Lord's Prayer)
- Luke 1:46–55 (Mary's Song of Praise – the Magnificat)

Consider the following Metrical Psalms and compare them with other versions, in scripture and elsewhere, such as the Gelineau Psalms. Are the psalms of the Scottish Psalter always worth preserving?

- Psalm 24:1–5 (tune: Tallis); Psalm 24:7–10 (tune: St George's Edinburgh)
- Psalm 23: compare with the hymn 'The King of Love my Shepherd is' and with the Gelineau version
- Psalm 109:21–25: is this the Word of God, good poetry or simply doggerel?
- Psalm 137 (tune: Old 137th): compare with No. 18 in *Songs of God's People* and the version in the musical *Godspell*.

## The Bible and the story of faith

We have already noted that the Bible is a widely varied body of literature, encompassing fact, fiction, fantasy, poetry and law. Through these various media, the story of the faith of a people is transmitted in such a way as to evoke from subsequent readers similar faith in God. For some church members, the suggestion that the Bible should be viewed as the literature of a devout people creates difficulties. The very idea that there is much in the Bible that is not factually accurate is, for some, a threat to faith. This need not, indeed should not, be so.

There is much in the Bible that purports to be history and which is both illuminating and helpful, but it must be read with care. Often, for example, the historical accounts given of the military conquests and defeats of Israel are completely one-sided. They are not only interpreted in a subjective manner but are given a religious gloss so that the mixed fortunes of the nation and its heroes are presented in the context of faith or faithlessness and obedience or disobedience. Everything is consequent upon fidelity to the Lord. No horrors are too great when inflicted upon the enemies of Israel and so rape, pillage and mutilation of the surrounding peoples are not only justified but projected as acts of faith and obedience to the divine will. So, reading such passages as Genesis 34 for concrete guidance is unlikely to be helpful!

There are, as hinted at earlier, numerous incidents recounted in the Bible for which conflicting accounts are given. There are even two versions of the Lord's Prayer which do not exactly square with one another; in Matthew 6:9–13 there are seven petitions but in Luke 11:2–4 there are only five petitions. Why *both* forms of the prayer were in general circulation in the Church at the same time requires explanation beyond the evidence of the Bible itself.

Much of the Bible has been categorised as myth, but what exactly is meant by that? It is a word which, in its modern, popular form, has been debased and come to mean something devoid of truth or reality. This is *not* what is meant by myth in relation to the Bible. The use of the term 'myth' can be explained by reference to the opening three chapters of Genesis where we find two distinct 'accounts' of creation: the *Priestly* teaching in Israel (the P code) and the teaching from the *Jahwehist* movement (or J code). There are two distinct forms of biblical myth and the creation stories offer an example of each.

Myth is what is said as certain religious rites are performed by and on behalf of the religious community. It declares in words what the ritual is designed to ensure through actions. For example, myth may be the words spoken in a sacrament. At the New Year festival in ancient Israel the triumph of order over chaos was relived by the community; it is believed that the great Creation Hymn of Genesis 1:1–2:4a was intoned. Unlike other creation hymns of its time, Genesis 1 is uncompromisingly monotheistic. There is only one God; when he speaks his Word is effective to create. The God of Genesis is not part of nature, nor to be equated with nature; he is the source of all life and transcends all existence. All of God's creation is good and acceptable, including humankind made in God's image. The idea of 'image' is fundamental here: it seems to mean that just as God is Lord over all creation, so man exercises under God a secondary lordship over the rest of creation (Psalm 8). Nevertheless, man is answerable to God for the way in which he exercises his lordship. This is the perception of the faith community that is revisited each year in the ritual and liturgy of the festival.

The second kind of myth is evident in Genesis 2:4b–3 and may be styled a 'story-myth' (or *aetiological myth*) in which many explanations of different depth may be offered within the one story. Probably, in this passage, there is evidence of two separate stories which have been harmonised. So we have two accounts of man placed in the garden (2:8 and 2:15), two accounts of the clothing of the man (3:7 and 3:21), two trees (the tree of life and the tree of good and evil) and so on. Yet the passage needs to be read as a whole. Answers to all kinds of questions are given: why the serpent is such an odd creature; why there is an instinctive antipathy between man and serpent; why there is pain in childbirth; why the farmer's lot is so hard; and why there is marriage and the different sexes.

Yet all these 'whys' are peripheral to the central thrust of the story. The heart of the story is theological: basic sin in man's nature mars his world. He is man, the rebel. He refuses to accept that he himself is not a god and not the centre of the universe. This passage, like Genesis 1, speaks of the greatness of humankind but the lordship portrayed – as Israel had every reason to reflect upon – is a marred lordship. The problem facing rebellious man was that of being reconciled with the Creator, and the faith story that unfolds subsequently throughout the Old Testament and into the New Testament is of lives seeking to turn friction into harmony with God.

These passages convey contrasting approaches and different theological nuances, as well as utilising different literary devices in the use of myth. That the myths convey fact is not always so, certainly not in the accounts of Genesis 1–3; that they convey deep *truth* is most certainly the case. Herein is the clue to the reading of much of the Bible.

In groups (20 minutes)

- What dangers do you see in using the Bible to support your point of view by proof-texting?
- Think of the way Paul presents his account of the Last Supper in 1 Corinthians 11:23–26. Is this a factual account or is it, in the sense discussed above, a myth? And does it matter?
- In an age when the Bible is seldom read outside a church service, does it matter?
- What value do you accord the faith stories of the Bible? How, where and when should they be read and taught?

# The God of the Bible

AIM

To promote the recognition that the Bible is quintessentially about God in human history.

STARTER

**Picturing God**

In earlier sessions much has been made of the Bible as the creation of people of faith and therefore as the product of human culture, ingenuity and piety. And so it is. For Christians, viewing the Bible through the eye of faith, the Bible is regarded as a primary means of the *revelation* of God and the purposes of God. In general terms, the Bible as a whole is interpreted as revealing or disclosing the divine nature and divine will. In specific terms, the Bible, primarily through the Gospels, reveals the nature and will of God in Jesus Christ.

Taking the Bible as a whole, we can consider the stories, poems and reflections of the Old and New Testaments as providing us with glimpses of what God is like. In a sense, they offer us snapshots of divinity. It would be foolish to claim that even in and through the Bible we can know all there is to know about God, but there is no doubt that for those who are ready to believe the essential propositions of a Christian doctrine of God, the Bible is full of clues; it offers us an enormous variety of insights which, taken together, enable us to picture something of what God is like. In so doing, the Bible elicits faith in the one true God from us. Indeed, this is its purpose.

## FOR REFLECTION AND DISCUSSION

In groups (20 minutes)

Consider the following passages and, using a flipchart, note in a few words the *images* of God that these snippets conjure up in your minds.

Genesis 1:1–3
Genesis 2:7
Genesis 3:8–10
Genesis 5:12–13; 17–18
Genesis 9:8–17
Genesis 11:5–9
Genesis 12:1–2
Genesis 22:13–17a
Genesis 41:25–32
Genesis 50:19–20

### The idea of God

It is possible to string together the references from Genesis and recognise some attributes of the God of the Hebrews that are central to the Christian idea of God. For example, there is the idea that God is *transcendent*; that is, above and beyond the natural world and not part of it, yet able to relate to the world of his creation. There is the notion of a personal God who involves himself in the life development of an individual. On a grander scale there is the idea of the God of history who forges dynasties and nations as a means of realising his long-term purpose for his entire creation. There is the idea of a God who is righteous but also who is merciful, a God who can destroy (for example, by flood) but also who can restore, renew and reinstate those who have been dispossessed. These and many more insights spring out of the Book of Genesis. Above all, there is the God who craves and demands allegiance. The people of faith *and* obedience are readily rewarded.

### The story of God as covenant

The Old Testament is, at the very least, the story of a people. It is also the story of that people's faith in God. Through that testimony we are able to piece together the developing story of God's dealings with his creation. Substantially, it is a story of *covenant* relationships. The idea of a covenant in the Old Testament was

one of promise or contract between two parties of unequal status, such as a chieftain and a member of his clan, or a lord and one of his serfs. Each pledged loyalty to the other. For example, the lord might pledge to protect and provide for his subject and the subject would pledge fealty and the readiness to fight under the banner of his lord. The notion of covenant is theologised in the Old Testament stories so that a deep, mystical and sacred tryst is entered into in which the element of benevolence and beneficence of God is supreme.

In groups (20 minutes)

Look at the notion of covenant in the following passages:

Genesis 7:17–18; 9:8–17
Genesis 15:18–21; 17:2–21
Exodus 2:23–25; 6:4–5
Exodus 24:1–8;
1 Chronicles 16:14–18

Discuss:

- What do the promises made in these passages have in common?
- What place does obedience have in the covenant?
- What does this covenant 'initiative' tell us about God?

Read together the story of the making of the Ark (or Box) of the Covenant) in Exodus 25:10–22. Use several English translations to get a fuller sense of the passage: the *Good News Bible* gives modern (metric) measurements but is bland and flat in its description whereas the *New English Bible* uses a richer and more majestic vocabulary in describing the piece.

List the features of the Box of the Covenant which interest you. What do these tell us of the Hebrew view of God?

### The presence of the Lord

In the Hebrew religion, the presence of the Lord in the midst of his people was everything to them. This is symbolised in their artefacts, their rituals and in their scriptures. Here are some examples of how the divine presence was represented:

- the bush that burns but is not consumed and the divine flame (Exodus 3:1–6)
- the holy mountain (Exodus 3:1, 19:3; see also 1 Kings 19:7–9, Isaiah 2:2–3a, Matthew 14:23; 17:1–3)
- the cloud (Exodus 13:17–22; 14:19)
- the tent of the presence (Exodus 26:1–36; 33:7–11)

When the Box of the Covenant, symbolising God's presence, was lost in a battle between the Philistines and the Israelites (1 Samuel 4:1–11) there was utter shame and desolation in Israel. The nation's leader, Eli, died from the shock of such devastating news (1 Samuel 4:12–18).

From such primitive beginnings there evolved a spiritualised concept of God's presence. Consider Ezekiel 1:1–3 and Psalm 139:7–12.

In groups (10 minutes)

Read the familiar story of the call of Isaiah in Isaiah 6:1–8. What does this suggest about having an awareness of God's presence?

**A personal God**

The stories of the heroes of Israel are interwoven with the development of a people and their self-understanding as a people of God. For great people of faith such as Abraham, David, Elijah and Jeremiah, not only is God the God of the faith community; he is a God with whom they feel a personal rapport. While the central theme of the Old Testament concerns the vocation of the people of Israel, very often this sense of vocation is particularised and initiated through the experience of a particular charismatic individual who has a profound, personal experience of the living God. Taken together, these stories provide a basis for a religion of personal encounter and for a deepening sense of personal spirituality.

Without question, this personalisation of the religious quest reaches its zenith in the life and ministry of Jesus of Nazareth. Even were we to look no further than Jesus' own personal quest, we soon become aware of the spiritual depth of Jesus as he wrestles with his own destiny.

In groups (15 minutes)

Discuss these episodes in the context of Jesus' growing awareness of his purpose and mission.

Matthew 3:13–17
Matthew 4:1–11
Matthew 16:13–20
Matthew 26:39, 42, 44
Matthew 27:46

## Paul's Letters and the story of God

Possibly one of the most significant events for the subsequent development of world history – and, unquestionably, for the development of the Christian religion – was the conversion of Saul of Tarsus. As Paul the apostle, he exercised astonishing influence over the primitive Church; through his teaching, he shaped in large measure the ways in which the Christian Church was to understand itself and its teachings. In the writings of Paul there is a robust, unflinching confidence both in the reality of God as *the* spiritual power in the universe and in the claim that 'God was in Christ, reconciling the world to himself' (2 Corinthians 5:19).

The Acts of the Apostles is a story of new beginnings and the development of a sectarian movement into an empire-wide Church. We read of those who were key figures in the expansion of the Jesus movement into something altogether new and different. Perhaps the most significant feature of the Acts is its report of the Jewish–Gentile conflict. The acceptance of non-Jews into the ranks of the faithful was of supreme importance for the survival and development of Christianity as a distinct religion. Without this acceptance, it is difficult to see how the Jesus movement could ever have been anything other than one more Jewish sect. Behind the Acts of the Apostles and the surviving letters of the first Christians, there is the conviction that the entire movement is God-inspired. The reference to the wisdom of Gamaliel (Acts 5:34) is significant. The author of Acts might as easily have entitled his work 'The Acts of the Spirit' or 'The Acts of God'.

The New Testament as a whole focuses on the overt power of God, evident in the lives of men and women who have experienced renewal in such exciting ways as to invite others to follow in their footsteps. When we come to ask, 'What is it we may trust about the Bible?' perhaps, above all, the answer has to do with trusting the forces of renewal, redirection and new purpose so evident in the first Christians. For Paul, the claim that 'If a person is in Christ (s)he is a new creation' (2 Corinthians 5:17) sums up the message of the New Testament.

**Can we trust the Bible?**

There is nothing magical about the Bible. It is a compendium of the writings of people of strong religious faith and great spiritual depth. The common thread running through it is the witness to the one true and living God. Through the language of remembered experience, of myth, of imaginative prophecy and of ecstasy we are offered not just a source book but a *resource*. For the believer who reads the Bible as Holy Scripture, there is a sense of the living quality of its message, a timeless and even contemporaneous ring to it.

To think of the Bible as 'the Word of God' seems perfectly legitimate. If by that phrase, however, we wish to convey that *everything* in the Bible is consistent with the will of God then that is manifestly not so. The issues raised by the nineteenth-century literalists and fundamentalists concerning the infallibility and inerrancy of the Bible as scripture belong to the downside of the history of biblical scholarship. The Bible has been as subject to human frailty and limitation as any other collection of writings. This does not in the least diminish its worth or its status as a work of immense spiritual and inspirational value. As for the relationship between God's Word and the Bible, the formula worked out by many churches in the Reformed tradition (the Church of Scotland among them) offers a helpful, if not altogether unambiguous, rule of thumb. That formula states that the Word of God *is contained in* the scriptures of the Old and New Testaments.

Each dimension in life has its own language, its own conceptual models and its own milieu. This is as true of religion as of the physical sciences, the social sciences, medicine or literature. The language of the Bible is a religious language. There is only one way to learn that language: to become immersed in it; to read the Bible in a spirit of openness and with a readiness to enter into the thought patterns of the various writers. Without that goodwill there can be no trust.

In groups (20 minutes)

- What do you make of the restrictive injunction in Revelation 22:18–19?
- Does it seem reasonable to you that the Bible should not include the testimony of great Christians in later centuries?
- Do you think that to deny the infallibility of the Bible and the inerrancy of scripture is to erode the authority of the Bible?
- Is the 'Word of God' confined to the Bible? Explain your answer.
- In what sense may the Bible be trusted today?